CW01512622

Original title:
Indigo Smiles Beyond the Phoenix Yawn

Copyright © 2025 Swan Charm
All rights reserved.

Author: Liisi Lendorav
ISBN HARDBACK: 978-1-80562-705-0
ISBN PAPERBACK: 978-1-80564-226-8

# The Last Petals of Twilight's Garden

In twilight's glow, the garden sighs,
A whispering breeze, where dreams arise.
Each petal falls like a gentle tear,
Embracing night, for the dawn draws near.

The moonlight dances on crimson leaves,
A cloak of secrets, the heart believes.
With shadows weaving through ancient trees,
Magic hums softly, carried by the breeze.

As fireflies flicker, a faint golden hue,
Stories unfold in the soft twilight blue.
Each flower holds a tale yet untold,
In the hush of the twilight, mysteries unfold.

Beneath the stars, where hopes take flight,
The last petals shimmer, kissed by night.
In silence they gather, dreams woven tight,
At the edge of darkness, preparing for light.

So linger a moment, in this sacred space,
Where time slows to gift us a quiet embrace.
For when dawn awakens, the petals will part,
But in twilight's garden, they'll stay in our heart.

### Awash in the Infinity of Light

In the vastness where dreams collide,
Stars whisper secrets, light does abide.
Colors dance in a timeless embrace,
Hope blooms gently in this sacred space.

Wisps of stardust on winds do play,
Guiding lost souls who've lost their way.
In every heartbeat, a glimmer of grace,
Awash in the beauty, time's tender trace.

## Transcendence of a Broken Dawn

Through shattered skies, the sun tries to peek,
Filling the silence with warmth so meek.
Each breath a promise, a chance to renew,
A canvas reborn with drops of dew.

The echoes of night, they whisper and fade,
Remnants of shadows in laughter displayed.
Golden horizons break dark's cruel hold,
In the heart of the brave, tales are retold.

## The Radiance After the Storm

After the tempest, the world holds its breath,
Washing away all remnants of death.
Raindrops like diamonds on leaves let them glisten,
Nature awakens, whispers listen.

The horizon glows with a soft, tender hue,
Painting the sky in shades ever new.
With each gentle breeze, old sorrows release,
In the light of renewal, there's silence and peace.

## Veils of Cosmic Laughter

Beneath the expanse where the cosmos twirls,
Veils of laughter weave in cosmic pearls.
Stars giggle softly in night's warm embrace,
Playing hide and seek in the vast open space.

Galaxies twinkle, their secrets unfold,
In the dance of the light, stories are told.
Each wink of a star, a jest from above,
A reminder of wonder, a gift wrapped in love.

### Fragments of Love in Twilight

In shadows deep, where whispers dwell,
Hearts entwined, casting a spell.
With every heartbeat, time stands still,
Lost in dreams, we feel the thrill.

The stars above, they softly shine,
Guiding paths that intertwine.
Moments fleeting, yet so bright,
Fragments of love in the twilight.

## Veils of Aether and Light

Through veils of mist, the dawn appears,
A symphony that calms our fears.
Dreams take flight on wings so fair,
For love awaits, beyond compare.

In the hush of morn, spirits soar,
Boundless magic, evermore.
With hearts ablaze, we chase the day,
Veils of aether lead the way.

## Radiance After the Ashes

From the remnants of our pain,
New hopes blossom, bright as rain.
In every tear, a story wakes,
Radiance forged from all heart aches.

Let the embers gently glow,
A fiery dance of love we'll know.
Through darkest nights, the dawn will rise,
Radiance blooms beneath the skies.

## Songs from a Celestial Abyss

In cosmic halls, where starlight sings,
Echoes of dreams, on silver wings.
A symphony of worlds unknown,
Songs from depths, forever grown.

Galaxies swirl, a dance divine,
In every note, our fates entwine.
Through the void, our spirits soar,
In the abyss, we crave for more.

# Ephemeral Shades of Tomorrow

In whispering winds, fate's shadows play,
Dancing like leaves in the light of day.
Colors that flicker, then fade from sight,
Chasing the moments that slip into night.

Words left unspoken, like secrets untold,
Fleeting as morning's first rays turn to gold.
Echoes of laughter on whispers of air,
A tapestry woven with delicate care.

Time folds like paper, frail dreams blend,
Each heartbeat a note in a song without end.
Fleeting for now, but forever they stay,
Ephemeral shades of tomorrow's ballet.

## The Rise of an Electric Dawn

Morning breaks softly, with hues of surprise,
A canvas of wonder, beneath waking skies.
Electric in colors, vibrant and bold,
A symphony of daylight, a story retold.

From slumbering shadows, the world comes alive,
Each moment ignites, like a fire to thrive.
Birds chirp their greetings, a jubilant choir,
Melodies swirling, lifting hearts higher.

Clouds drift like dreams on the cusp of the morn,
Painting the heavens, a canvas reborn.
As golden rays shimmer, igniting the dawn,
Hope rises gently, a promise drawn on.

### Dreamcatchers in a Vivid Night

Under a blanket of starlit embrace,
Whispers of dreams in a mystical space.
Weaving through shadows, the stories unfold,
Dreamcatchers glimmer with tales yet untold.

Winds carry secrets on silken threads tight,
Capturing wishes that dance in the night.
In kaleidoscope visions, where fantasies soar,
Hearts find their rhythm, longing for more.

Moonbeams caress, with a delicate hand,
Guiding lost dreams to find where they stand.
In vivid enchantment, where magic ignites,
We gather our hopes, 'neath the canvas of nights.

## Horizon's Kiss with an Open Heart

Where the sky meets the sea, a promise is made,
A horizon's kiss, where shadows won't fade.
With an open heart, let the adventure begin,
Embrace what awaits, as the new day spins.

Footsteps on sand, with stories to share,
The echoes of laughter carried by air.
Waves sing a ballad, a timeless refrain,
Of love and of loss, of joy and of pain.

Nature's sweet brush paints a scene so divine,
Where hope chases dreams, like the stars that align.
With arms open wide, to the sky we will sway,
In horizon's sweet kiss, we find our way.

# The Whisper of Stars in Twilight

In twilight's hush, the stars take flight,
They whisper secrets, soft and light.
The moon, a sentinel, watches near,
While dreams unfurl, banishing fear.

In silver pools of shimmering glow,
The world awakens, spirits flow.
A lullaby of night weaves tight,
As shadows dance, embracing night.

With every twinkle, tales are spun,
Of ancient realms and battles won.
Their voice is gentle, yet profound,
In cosmic rhythm, hope is found.

Through velvet skies, like echoes, fade,
Our hearts entwined in twilight's shade.
For in this stillness, we become,
One with the stars, our souls as one.

## Beneath the Veil of Cosmic Dreams

Beneath the veil of dreams so vast,
Where time and space are lightly cast,
Galaxies whisper in muted tones,
Reminding us we're never alone.

In cosmic gardens, starlight blooms,
We trace our hopes through silver tombs.
Each sparkling grain, a wish sent high,
In the cradle of night, where memories lie.

Nebulae dance in celestial play,
Our spirits soar, drifting away.
With every heartbeat, a story we weave,
In the fabric of night, we learn to believe.

Through shimmering pathways, we dare to roam,
Finding our light in the darkness, our home.
Beneath the veil, we seek our fate,
In the cosmos, we contemplate.

## The Journey Through Prismatic Winds

Through prismatic winds, we take to flight,
Each color a whisper, brilliant and bright.
With every breeze, a path unfolds,
In a tapestry woven with tales of old.

The clouds, like dreams, drift soft and free,
Carrying echoes of the great sea.
We follow the currents, our hearts alight,
With a song of hope, igniting the night.

As sun-kissed rays break through the gray,
We paint the skies, come what may.
For in this journey, we find our way,
Embracing the winds that dance and sway.

With every gust, our fears take flight,
In the journey of souls, we ignite.
Through prismatic winds, our spirits sing,
Chasing the dreams that freedom can bring.

## Ethereal Light Beyond the Horizon

At dawn's first blush, beyond the horizon,
Ethereal light begins its season.
Soft colors merge, as day awakes,
Whispers of magic in each breath it takes.

In golden beams, the world expands,
Guiding our hearts with gentle hands.
The sun, a guardian, rises high,
Bestowing warmth as dreams comply.

Beneath this light, our hopes ignite,
Through every shadow, we chase the light.
With quiet courage, we move ahead,
In the glow of the dawn, our fears are shed.

Beyond the horizon, the future gleams,
In the morning's embrace, we nurture our dreams.
Ethereal light, our guiding star,
Promises whispering, we've come so far.

## Portrait of Dreams in the Ether

In twilight's grasp, the shadows blend,
Whispers of hopes that softly bend.
A canvas bright with starlit thread,
Where wishes linger, never dead.

Each breath of night, a story spun,
Of battles fought, and victories won.
Through vibrant hues the heart can soar,
Unlocking realms forevermore.

From glimmering dust, the visions rise,
In quiet corners, under skies.
A tapestry of light and grace,
We wander through this sacred space.

With every stroke, a nebula blooms,
A dance of magic in shadowed rooms.
Where dreams collide with starlit beams,
And hope unfolds in silver streams.

So paint your dreams in colors bold,
A portrait of the tales untold.
In ether's embrace, let hearts ignite,
And find the dawn beyond the night.

## The Celestial Bloom after Ruin

Amidst the ashes, a whisper grows,
A fragile seed where courage flows.
From rubble vast, a flower sparks,
In twilight's hush, defying dark.

With petals soft as evening's breath,
It dances lightly near the death.
Each bloom a tale of strength reborn,
A symphony for souls once torn.

In the silence of forgotten fields,
The universe's beauty yields.
From grief and night, a spectrum springs,
And in that light, the heart takes wings.

Stars twinkle bright above the strain,
As roots entwine through love and pain.
A testament of life's own grace,
The bloom will rise, we'll find our place.

Embrace the cycle, joy and gloom,
For in the heart lives hope's own bloom.
In each new dawn, a chance to feel,
A promise made, a fate to seal.

## Voices of the Forgotten Spectrum

In shadows deep, the voices wane,
Echoes soft of joy and pain.
A spectrum ranges far and wide,
Yet seldom heard, they now reside.

They whisper stories lost in time,
In colors bright, a silent rhyme.
Reflections of a world unseen,
Where laughter mingles with the keen.

From muted hues, a symphony,
Calls forth the past with reverie.
Each chord of memory softly plays,
A dance of light through hidden days.

As twilight falls, the spirits rise,
With gentle notes that touch the skies.
Their legacy, a gentle sigh,
A reminder that we too can fly.

So listen close, for life's refrain,
Is but a thread through joy and pain.
In every hue, a voice will sing,
To tell of peace and hope they bring.

# A Journey Through Celestial Tides

Upon the waves of starlit seas,
We sail on winds, a whispered breeze.
With cosmic charts, our hearts aligned,
To realms untouched, a fate designed.

Through swirling mists, the journey calls,
In depths of night, adventure sprawls.
With every crest, a new delight,
And in each trough, the unknown's flight.

We dance with comets, weave with stars,
Embracing dreams beyond our scars.
The universe, a vast expanse,
In every moment, we find our chance.

With navigation set by heart,
We chart a course where wonders start.
The tide may shift, the stars may swirl,
Yet in this dance, the cosmos twirl.

So let us drift, no course in mind,
Through stardust realms, our spirits blind.
In celestial tides, we find our way,
As night turns bright, and dawn holds sway.

## The Harmony of Celestial Hearts

In the quiet of the twilight sky,
Stars whisper secrets, floating by.
Moonbeams cradle dreams anew,
While nightingales sing a song just for you.

With every twinkle an echo of grace,
Hearts entwined in this wondrous space.
Cosmic rhythms dance in time,
Surging through realms, sublime and prime.

Fleeting moments wrapped in light,
Guided gently by the night.
Together we weave a tapestry bright,
In the heart's embrace, taking flight.

Celestial bodies, a grand ballet,
Guiding lost souls along the way.
With laughter and love, we shall unite,
Under the velvet, starry night.

# Awakening the Dream Weaver

In caverns deep where shadows dwell,
Lies the Dream Weaver with tales to tell.
With threads of silver and dreams spun bright,
She calls forth magic from the night.

With every stitch, a vision flows,
Enchanting journeys where no one knows.
Whispers of wonders softly beckon,
In the fragile dawn, her magic's reckoned.

Through realms of dreams, we wander free,
With colors dancing on the winds of glee.
A tapestry woven in the midnight hour,
Revealing the dreams that hold us with power.

Each sigh a spark, each thought a thread,
A narrative rising from where dreams are bred.
In shimmering light, the heart takes flight,
Awakening visions woven in the night.

## Metamorphosis in a Glassy Reflection

In mirrors deep like pools of time,
Shadows flicker as thoughts entwine.
Faces change, yet spirits remain,
In glassy reflections, we feel the strain.

Transformation whispers through the air,
Beauty lies hidden, it's always there.
With every glance, the soul will mend,
Unlocking the truths we must defend.

Ripples ripple in the starlit glow,
Revealing secrets that we must know.
In the depths of silence, our essence grows,
Moments captured as the river flows.

Through glassy reflections, we dance and spin,
Finding ourselves where journeys begin.
Amid metamorphosis, we learn to see,
The beauty in change, embracing the free.

## Sparks of Laughter at Dusk

As daylight fades to a soft embrace,
Laughter twinkles in a warm space.
Children giggle beneath the trees,
In the golden hour, carried by the breeze.

Each spark of joy lights up the night,
Painting shadows with sheer delight.
Whispers share ancient tales of old,
In the fading light, their magic's bold.

With every chuckle, the heart's aglow,
Illuminating paths where dreams can flow.
Under the stars, the world unites,
In joyous harmony, we reach new heights.

The dusk holds laughter, wild and true,
In its fleeting moment, a world anew.
Together, we revel in this magical time,
Where sparks of laughter are the purest rhyme.

## Chasing Shadows of a Vibrant Past

Footsteps linger on cobblestones,
Echoes of laughter, whispers of tone.
In sunlit glades where dreams collide,
Memories weave like an endless tide.

Fragments of time, a tapestry spun,
Where youth was bright, and shadows run.
Chasing the echoes, we dare to tread,
In realms of the heart, where spirits are fed.

Old photographs, a window to then,
In shadows, we find our little suns.
Though years may fade like the evening light,
The colors of joy emerge from the night.

A garden where wishes bloom anew,
Each petal a tale of what's tried and true.
In the quiet, we find the key,
Unlocking the doors of what used to be.

And so we wander through realms of gold,
Chasing shadows that never grow old.
In the vibrant past, we find our place,
In the flicker of time, we embrace our grace.

# The Dance of Dusk and Hope

In the twilight where shadows blend,
Hope emerges as daylight ends.
Stars awaken in soft embrace,
A gentle hush, a tranquil space.

Twinkling fires in a velvet sky,
Whispers of dreams that dare to fly.
Each flicker tells of battles fought,
Of glimmers found in what we sought.

The moon hangs low, a guardian bright,
Warding off shadows with silver light.
Dancing whispers touch the air,
A symphony woven with love and care.

Beneath the stars, hearts intertwine,
In the fading light, our spirits align.
With every step, we boldly share,
The dance of dusk, a tale laid bare.

And in the silence, hope does thrive,
Murmurs of promise, we come alive.
In the heart of night, magic does cope,
With every heartbeat, we dance with hope.

## Wings of Azure Thinking

Thoughts take flight on sapphire skies,
Winged dreams soaring, where freedom lies.
In azure realms, the mind does roam,
Finding the whispers that call us home.

Each moment glimmers, a promise bright,
Ideas alight like stars in the night.
With crayon colors, we sketch with glee,
The wings of thinking, wild and free.

Breezes carry our hopes afar,
As we chart paths beneath a guiding star.
In realms of wonder, beyond the hue,
Our imaginations take flight anew.

So let us rise on the winds of thought,
To places of solace, blissfully sought.
With wings of azure, hearts overflowing,
We dance through the skies, forever knowing.

In every dream, let courage stay,
For the wings of thinking will light the way.
In vibrant breaths, we claim the skies,
With wings unfurled, our spirits rise.

# Reveries of the Celestial Dawn

As the night surrenders to golden seams,
The celestial dawn whispers of dreams.
Colors cascade like a painter's brush,
Awakening hearts in the morning hush.

In soft pastels, the world is reborn,
With dew-kissed petals, and the light of morn.
Every moment wrapped in a tender glow,
The magic of life begins to flow.

Through pastel hues, we find our way,
Guided by hope that starts the day.
Each sunrise carries a promise so bright,
Reveries blossom in the gentle light.

With open arms, we greet the sky,
In awe of the wonders that drift on high.
In the warmth of dawn, we stand enthralled,
In celestial dreams where spirits are called.

So let us cherish these moments divine,
In the embrace of dawn, our souls entwine.
For in each sunrise, new journeys are sworn,
In reveries sweet, our hearts will be worn.

## Awakening Soft Tones of Hope

In dawn's embrace, the world anew,
Soft hues emerge from skies so blue.
The whispers call of dreams untold,
As hearts awaken, brave and bold.

With every breath, the promise swells,
In secret glades where magic dwells.
The petals bloom, the songs resound,
In nature's arms, our hope is found.

So let the light, like rivers flow,
Through tangled woods where fairies glow.
In every shadow, there lies a spark,
A tale reborn from gentle dark.

With every step, the path defined,
Unravel mysteries left behind.
In whispered winds, our spirits dance,
In twilight's glow, we take a chance.

The morning sun, a golden guide,
Awakens dreams we cannot hide.
In joyous laughter, troubles cease,
And every heart finds sweet release.

## Between Stars and Shadows

In twilight's veil, where secrets play,
The stars align in grand ballet.
With every wish upon the night,
Hope flickers gently, burning bright.

Across the sky, the whispers weave,
Tales of wonder, hearts believe.
In shadows deep, where fears reside,
The light of courage must abide.

Between each star, a story lies,
Of fleeting dreams and endless skies.
Through darkened paths, we won't despair,
For love will find us everywhere.

With every heartbeat, fate conspires,
Igniting souls like ancient fires.
In cosmic dance, we take our place,
Bound by the stars, embraced in grace.

So let us soar, though shadows loom,
For in our hearts, there's always room.
Between the stars, we reach for light,
In unity, we shine so bright.

## Luminescent Whispers on the Wind

In quiet moments, soft and clear,
The whispers of the night draw near.
They carry tales of days long past,
Of dreams that linger, shadows cast.

Beneath the moon, the world aglow,
Each breath of wind begins to flow.
With every turn, a secret told,
A promise wrapped in silver gold.

Through rustling leaves, and swaying trees,
The echoes dance upon the breeze.
In every sigh, in every tone,
A symphony of hearts, alone.

And when the dawn begins to break,
The whispers weave through every lake.
They sing of hope, of love so true,
Of morning skies in vibrant blue.

So heed those soundless calls you hear,
For magic waits with patience here.
The luminescent lights will guide,
To dreams awakened, hearts wide-eyed.

# Resurgence at the Edge of Night

When dusk descends with velvet grace,
A dance of shadows finds its place.
The moon ascends, a silver eye,
In quiet moments, dreams can fly.

Through whispering winds, the past takes flight,
Resurgence stirs at the edge of night.
In darkened corners, secrets bloom,
And nature hums a soft, sweet tune.

Each heartbeat echoes in the dark,
A tale of hope, a distant spark.
With every star that sketches light,
We rise again, embracing night.

The world awakens from its rest,
In glossy leaves, our spirits blessed.
Through every fear, we bravely stride,
Together, hearts forever tied.

As dawn approaches, gently found,
The night's embrace will still resound.
For in the end, we find our way,
Resurgence blooms at break of day.

## Whispers of Twilight Hues

In twilight's soft embrace, we stroll,
The shadows dance, the evening's toll.
A whisper speaks from the fading light,
As stars awaken, taking flight.

The colors blend, a soft caress,
With every shade, a gentle press.
The moon begins its nightly climb,
A silver thread through bated time.

Each sigh of wind, a secret shared,
In quiet corners, hearts laid bare.
The twilight's magic lingers long,
In whispered tales, we find our song.

Soft mists weave tales of yesteryear,
Fleeting moments, vividly clear.
In hues of purple, gold, and teal,
The heart's true wishes we conceal.

As darkness falls, we take our leave,
With twilight's whispers, we believe.
A canvas vast, where dreams unite,
In whispered twilight, hearts ignite.

# Sapphire Echoes at Dawn

The dawn awakens, hues of blue,
A sapphire sky, a world anew.
Birds in chorus, sweetly sing,
As light unfolds, a joyous spring.

The dewdrops glisten on emerald leaves,
In gentle breezes, nature weaves.
Each whisper tells of night's retreat,
Of dreams that danced on phantom feet.

The sun, a brush, begins to paint,
A canvas bright, a vivid saint.
With every stroke, the world ignites,
In sapphire echoes, day invites.

A journey starts with morning's grace,
As shadows fade, we find our place.
In light's embrace, we rise and soar,
With sapphire echoes, forevermore.

The horizon glows with golden hue,
Each moment cherished, fresh and true.
In radiant realms where hopes are spun,
The day unfolds, our song begun.

### The Resilient Palette of Dawn

In dawn's embrace, colors ignite,
A palette bright, a wondrous sight.
Each brushstroke bold, yet soft and kind,
Awakening dreams, once confined.

Through storms we've trekked, through shadows cast,
Resilient hearts, our shadows passed.
With every hue, a story blooms,
In morning's light, dispelling glooms.

The whispers of night begin to fade,
A canvas vast, where fears invade.
Yet, here we stand, with spirits strong,
In vibrant shades, where we belong.

With every stroke, the past gives way,
To brighter tomorrows, come what may.
The dawn ignites, we paint our fate,
In resilient hues, we elevate.

In laughter, love, in every tone,
The palette sings, we are not alone.
With morning's blush, hope's light we seek,
In vibrant colors, we are unique.

# Wings of a Midnight Dream

In the cloak of night, dreams take flight,
On whispered wings, in silken light.
The moon unveils its silver glow,
As shadows dance, we gently flow.

Each star a story, old yet new,
In midnight's grasp, we wander through.
With every heartbeat, magic breathes,
In silent realms, where heart believes.

Beneath the heavens, we float and soar,
On wings of dreams, forevermore.
A tapestry of thoughts unspun,
In midnight's cradle, we're all one.

With starlit whispers, secrets speak,
In moonlit laughter, we find the peak.
Each moment lingers, rich and sweet,
As midnight dreams and daylight greet.

As dawn approaches, shadows flee,
Yet in our hearts, the dreams will be.
With every twilight, pathways gleam,
On wings of hope, we boldly dream.

## Whispers of Twilight Wings

In the hush of twilight's kiss,
Soft shadows dance and twist,
Beneath the fading light,
A world begins to drift.

Feathered phantoms take their flight,
On whispered winds of night,
Each flutter sings a tale,
Of dreams that soar and sail.

Stars awaken in the deep,
Guarding secrets they must keep,
A tapestry above,
Woven with ancient love.

Moonlight bathes the earth in glow,
As rivers of silver flow,
Guiding hearts toward the hazy
Adventures that feel so crazy.

With every breath, the night unfolds,
Magic in its gentle hold,
For in the dark, we find our spark,
Whispered hopes that light the dark.

# Echoes in the Amethyst Sky

Underneath the violet dome,
Where dreams and wishes roam,
The echoes of the past resound,
Revealing truths profound.

In twilight's gentle grasp we stand,
With secrets spilling from the sand,
Every shadow holds a story,
Bathed in reminiscence and glory.

The stars align for tales untold,
As moonbeams weave their threads of gold,
In whispers soft, longings sigh,
Echoing through the amethyst sky.

With every heartbeat, fate aligns,
In cosmic dance, the heart entwines,
In silence blooms a soft refrain,
Of love and loss, of joy and pain.

And as the night begins to fade,
We hold the memories we've made,
In every color, every hue,
The echoes sing: we live anew.

# Dreams Bathed in Cerulean Hues

Upon the canvas of the morn,
Where dawn's bright colors are reborn,
The cerulean expanse unfolds,
As whispered dreams begin to hold.

In every shade of azure glow,
Imagination starts to flow,
Each thought a sail upon the breeze,
Floating softly through the trees.

Clouds like cotton candy drift,
Carrying hopes when spirits lift,
In the sky's unending sea,
We find our true identity.

With every heartbeat, dreams arise,
Reflecting beauty in our eyes,
In this world of endless blue,
Every vision feels more true.

As sunlight spills, a gentle grace,
We find our way, we find our place,
In the cerulean embrace,
We dance with joy, and time we chase.

# The Awakening of Dawn's Laughter

As dawn peeks through the shroud of night,
With laughter that brings pure delight,
It chases shadows, deep and long,
Awakening the world with song.

Each ray of light, a gentle tease,
Whispers through the boughs of trees,
With every giggle, life is born,
In the glistening dew of morn.

The flowers stretch, the colors bloom,
In harmony, dispelling gloom,
For in the laughter, joy will spring,
As nature wakes and begins to sing.

The sun emerges, bold and free,
Filling hearts with hope, you see,
In dawn's embrace, we find our way,
In laughter's light, we greet the day.

So let us dance, let spirits soar,
In the awakening, forevermore,
For every laugh, a spark ignites,
A promise in the morning's light.

## Fragments of Light in Night's Embrace

In shadows deep, the stars do gleam,
A whispering glow, a fleeting dream.
Through twilight's shroud, they flicker bright,
Fragments of hope in the arms of night.

A silver shaft on dew-kissed grass,
Where whispers of time like shadows pass.
Gentle caress of the moon's soft hand,
Guiding lost souls to a promised land.

Each twinkle tells a tale untold,
Of journeys brave and hearts of gold.
In the embrace of the muted dark,
The world alights with a fiery spark.

Yet darkness holds a magic rare,
A veil that dances, a lingering air.
As night retreats with dawn's first sigh,
Fragile moments soar to the sky.

The dreamers wait with hearts in flight,
Collecting fragments of fading night.
In every glimmer, a story lies,
A bridge to worlds beyond our skies.

# Hope's Flame in a Dusky Realm

When day retreats, and shadows creep,
A softer glow begins to seep.
In dusky realms where wishes hang,
Hope's flame flickers, tender and sang.

The nightingale sings a wistful tune,
Under the watchful gaze of the moon.
Each note, a promise, carried so far,
Guiding lost hearts like a guiding star.

Though darkness looms, its grip is light,
Illuminated by dreams so bright.
In each twilight breath, a chance to find,
A spark of joy within the blind.

For every sorrow the shadows sow,
Hope, like a river, continues to flow.
With courage wrapped in a silken fold,
Life's tapestry weaves stories bold.

Thus in the dusk, with embers aglow,
United we stand, against the shadow.
Ever steady, through time's embrace,
Hope's flame ignites, illuminating grace.

# The Echo of Celestial Lullabies

In the stillness of night, a hymn takes flight,
Carried by whispers of cosmic light.
Each note a shimmer, a distant call,
Echoes of lullabies to cradle us all.

The stars, like children, twinkle and play,
Casting their magic in a heavenly array.
Their melodies weave through darkened skies,
Secrets of wonder hidden in sighs.

As dreams unfurl beneath gentle stars,
The universe speaks of who we are.
Each breath a promise, each sigh a wish,
In cosmic pools, our souls they swish.

Awash in dreams, like waves on the sea,
These lullabies cradle both you and me.
In celestial arms we find our peace,
A quiet moment where worries cease.

So close your eyes and listen near,
To echoes of love that whisper clear.
In the arms of night, we'll drift and sway,
To the lullabies of the Milky Way.

# Radiant Memories at Dusk

As the sun dips low, the world aglow,
Memories linger, soft and slow.
Each radiant hue tells tales once spun,
Of laughter shared, of friendships won.

In the quiet hour where shadows blend,
Time dances softly, a gentle friend.
With every sigh, a moment treks,
Carried on breezes, like gentle specks.

The twilight paints a canvas grand,
Of moments cherished, both close at hand.
In the embrace of dusk's warm kiss,
We find the whispers of simple bliss.

As stars appear, like diamonds bright,
They hold the fragments of day's sweet light.
Catching our dreams in nets of gold,
Radiant memories, forever bold.

So let us gather these twilight gems,
In the heart's chest, where yearning stems.
As day bids farewell, and night takes flight,
We treasure the memories held so tight.

# Chasing Reflections of Stardust

In shadows cast by silver beams,
We weave our dreams on whispering streams.
With every glance our spirits rise,
Chasing reflections, beneath starry skies.

The night unfolds its velvet cloak,
Where secrets linger, and silence spoke.
We wander paths of glittered light,
Embracing wonder in the night's flight.

Each star a story, a tale untold,
Of glimmered hopes and hearts that bold.
We dance in circles, hand in hand,
A tapestry spun in a twilight land.

With every wish upon the breeze,
We find our solace among the trees.
For stardust calls with a gentle sigh,
Nurtured dreams soar, as time slips by.

In the soft embrace of the Milky Way,
We chase reflections and lose our way.
But in the chaos of cosmic embrace,
We find our light, our rightful place.

# The Awakening of Skyward Hearts

Through morning mist, the sun shall rise,
Awakening hearts beneath vast skies.
With open wings, we greet the day,
In harmony's dance, we find our way.

The song of birds, a sweet refrain,
Echoing softly through the lane.
With laughter woven in the air,
We cast our worries, divest our care.

In budding blooms, the promise grows,
Each gentle petal whispers so.
With every heartbeat, we are free,
Bound to the heavens, just you and me.

As sunlight bathes the waking world,
Our spirits soar, unflagging, unfurled.
With dreams that flutter in morning's glow,
Together we rise, together we flow.

In the gentle dawn, love's light ignites,
The awakening of skyward sights.
With every moment, our souls entwined,
In this beautiful journey, joyfully aligned.

## Harmony in the Midnight Hour

When stars align in velvet skies,
We find our truth where silence lies.
In shadows deep, our whispers twine,
The midnight hour, a sacred sign.

With stars our compass, we navigate,
Through dreams uncharted, we celebrate.
In every heartbeat, a symphony plays,
Through the quiet, our spirits blaze.

The moon, a guardian, watches near,
Its silver glow, our hearts endear.
With every sigh, a rhythm unfurls,
In harmony, we dance in whirls.

Beneath the canvas of twinkling lights,
We share our secrets, our lofty heights.
In the embrace of night's sweet song,
Together we thrive, together we belong.

As dawn approaches with whispers low,
We hold onto the magic, let it flow.
In the midnight hour, we find our grace,
In the beauty of this enchanting space.

# Tender Blues of Fleeting Days

In tender hues, the daylight fades,
We watch the sun as it serenades.
With every moment, a memory stays,
In the gentle blues of fleeting days.

The wind whispers secrets of yore,
While shadows dance by the open door.
With laughter shared and stories spun,
In gentle twilight, we find our fun.

As stars emerge, a soft embrace,
We seek the warmth in the evening's grace.
With hands held tight beneath the sky,
In fleeting days, together we fly.

The horizon blushes, a painter's dream,
In every sunset, love's golden gleam.
We treasure moments, brief yet bright,
In tender blues, we find our light.

With every sigh, the night descends,
And in the stillness, our hearts transcend.
Together we weave the fabric of time,
In the tender blues, our lives rhyme.

## Celestial Notes in the Aether

In the hush of the twilight's embrace,
Stars weave stories in silent space.
Whispers drift on the gentle breeze,
Carrying secrets from ancient trees.

The moon hums softly a calming tune,
Crystals shimmer like dust from the moon.
Constellations dance in an endless waltz,
Reminding us all of the vastness that vaults.

In this realm where the dreams take flight,
We find our solace in endless night.
Each breath a note in the cosmic song,
A melody pure, where we all belong.

Galaxies spiral in vibrant embrace,
Drawing us into their spiraled grace.
Bound by the threads of fate's tender weave,
We dare to hope and we dare to believe.

With each dawn, let the visions renew,
As celestial notes guide us on through.
The heart's compass points to the skies,
Where even the most daring dreamers rise.

# Harmonics of Phoenix Flight

With wings of fire, oh, how we soar,
Across the horizon, forevermore.
The air crackles with whispers of light,
As dreams awaken in the heart of night.

In the warmth of hope, the shadows flee,
A symphony echoes, wild and free.
Every note is a feather, bright,
Carving the dusk with pure delight.

Through valleys deep, where the sorrows dwell,
We rise above, breaking every spell.
Our spirits alight, like the sun's own fire,
We dance to the song of our own desire.

On currents of time, we glide and we spin,
Life's harmonics begin to begin.
In the glow of embers, we find our voice,
In the heartbeat of love, we all rejoice.

Thus, let us soar on wings broad and wide,
With the phoenix guiding, our constant guide.
In the echoes of night, our souls ignite,
Creating a legacy, pure and bright.

## The Mirage of Lapis Dreams

In the twilight's grasp, where shadows dwell,
A mirage flickers, casting its spell.
Lapis lazuli skies stretch far and near,
Holding secrets only dreamers can hear.

Each droplet of azure whispers a tale,
Of magic and wonder beyond the pale.
In this realm of imagination's gleam,
We chase the elusive, the lapis dream.

Ripples of sapphire in the moonlit stream,
Reflecting the hopes of a tender dream.
Underneath the cosmos, we drift and glide,
On waves of stardust, we ebb and ride.

Finding solace in the nebulous sway,
As colors blend in a mystical way.
Lost in the depths of the night's embrace,
Time slows, revealing another place.

In visions vibrant, we learn to believe,
In the whispers of night, we grieve and weave.
The lapis dreams blend reality's seam,
Awakening the heart to the wonders we glean.

## Marigold Futures in a Refracted Sky

Beneath a canopy of marigold glow,
Futures dance like the petals that blow.
With hues of sunset, they whisper of fate,
In the garden of time, where hopes cultivate.

Each dawn a promise, a canvas anew,
Where dreams are painted in golden hue.
In the light that refracts, shadows disperse,
Nurturing visions, we dare to immerse.

As sunlight stretches across the wide land,
We find our footing, take life by the hand.
Choices like seeds in the fertile ground,
With each kind act, new futures abound.

Through storms that may come, we weather with grace,
Harvesting laughter in this sacred space.
The echoes of joy in the marigold fields,
Reveal the abundance true love yields.

So let us wander in this refracted light,
Chasing our dreams, with hearts burning bright.
With marigold futures, may we always rise,
Crafting our paths beneath vastening skies.

## Tales Carried on the Celestial Tide

Whispers of the moonlit sea,
From realms beyond our sight,
Carried forth by dreams that fly,
To cradle stars in the night.

Waves that dance on velvet shores,
Tell tales of wishes past,
In their ebb and flow, they sing,
Of futures that are vast.

Fleeting shadows drift and weave,
Through currents soft and deep,
Each secret held within the tide,
A promise theirs to keep.

The ocean's heart forever swells,
With echoes from afar,
As starlight spills in silver trails,
To light the evening's hour.

Journey forth, dear sailor bold,
Embrace the night's sweet air,
For in these tides of travel wide,
All souls are free to dare.

## Serenade of the Awakening Sky

Dawn's soft blush ignites the day,
As shadows yield to light,
The world awakens, fresh and new,
In colors pure and bright.

Birds take flight in melodies,
Their songs weave through the trees,
A serenade that lifts our hearts,
On gentle morning breeze.

Clouds, like dreams, drift lazily,
In hues of gold and blue,
Each moment whispers magic sweet,
As daylight breaks in view.

The sun's embrace, a warm caress,
Unfolds the day anew,
With every beam, with every ray,
The world is born in hue.

Awake now, spirits bright and bold,
Embrace the joy anew,
For in this serenade of sky,
Life's wonders come to you.

# Chasing Echoes of the Iridescent

In twilight's glow, where dreams take flight,
We chase the echoes bright,
Through forests deep and rivers wide,
In shadows kissed by light.

Colors dance in fleeting forms,
Like whispers on the breeze,
Each shimmer holds a story lost,
In twilight's gentle tease.

With laughter bright, we wander free,
Upon the paths of fate,
As mysteries of twilight bloom,
Within the hands of fate.

The world transforms in shades divine,
As stars begin to gleam,
We capture memories, fleeting soft,
Like echoes of a dream.

So let us chase what shimmered bright,
In moments held so dear,
For in the dance of iridescent light,
We find what we hold near.

# The Resilience of Morning's Embrace

Morning sun in tender grace,
Breaks the night's old spell,
With every beam, a new chance born,
In whispers soft, we dwell.

Through trials faced and tears once shed,
The heart learns how to soar,
In hope reborn with each new dawn,
The spirit seeks for more.

Petals glisten with the dew,
In gardens waking slow,
Each bloom a testament of strength,
To dreams that ebb and flow.

Resilience flows like rivers deep,
With currents strong and bold,
In every ending, beginnings lie,
A treasure to behold.

So rise, dear soul, with morning bright,
Embrace the light's warm call,
For in the dawn's sweet embrace,
We rise, we stand, we fall.

## Beyond the Ember's Last Breath

In twilight's embrace, shadows dance slow,
Whispers of magic, the secrets they know.
Embers flicker bright, a hearth's gentle sigh,
As night wraps the world in a soft, darkened tie.

Each star like a tear, in the velvet sky,
Holds stories of dreams that will never die.
Time drifts like smoke, where the lost shadows tread,
Carried by silence, the words left unsaid.

Through remnants of flame, the phoenix will rise,
With feathers of gold that ignite the night skies.
In echoes of warmth, in echoes of grace,
The ember's last breath finds a new, sacred place.

Luminous hearts weave a tapestry rare,
From the ashes of woe, to the brilliance laid bare.
In twilight's embrace, we find hope reborn,
Beyond ember's last glow, a new dawn is sworn.

So linger awhile, in this magical haze,
Where time holds its breath, lost in timeless praise.
We'll gather the starlight, forever interlace,
Beyond the ember's last breath, find warmth in the space.

# The Crescendo of Morning's Breath


With dawn's gentle fingers, the night whispers low,
The chorus of dreams bids a soft, sweet hello.
Birds burst into song, as if time held its bow,
In the crescendo of morning, the world starts to glow.

The dew-kissed petals, awake to the sun,
Each drop like a diamond, a new day begun.
With laughter of children, the air is alive,
In the magic of moments, the spirits will thrive.

Clouds dance in the sky, a ballet so fair,
The breeze hums its tune, a melodious flare.
Nature's own symphony, rising like breath,
In the crescendo of morning, we cast off our death.

Together we wander, through fields kissed with light,
As shadows retreat into remnants of night.
With whispers of hope, the universe sings,
In the crescendo of morning, new life softly springs.

Let's gather these moments, our hearts interlace,
In the glow of the morning, there's magic, there's grace.
For with every sunrise, there's magic anew,
In the crescendo of morning, our dreams will come true.

## Reflections of Turquoise Joy

In the depths of the sea, where secrets do dwell,
Turquoise waves curl softly, casting their spell.
The laughter of dolphins, a sparkling gleam,
In the reflections of water, we float and we dream.

The sun dances lightly on each rippling crest,
Carrying whispers, as nature finds rest.
With each playful splash, like the heart's sweet delight,
In reflections of turquoise, we bask in pure light.

From coral-built kingdoms, the tales that they weave,
In hues rich and deep, like threads we believe.
The tide sings of stories, from ages gone by,
In the warmth of their colors, the echoes can fly.

With arms open wide, we embrace every wave,
In the dance of the sea, we find what we crave.
Together we gather the joy of our hearts,
In the reflections of turquoise, where wonder imparts.

So carry this spirit, let it kiss your soul,
For within the blue depths, we find we are whole.
Turquoise joy beckons, a vibrant embrace,
In reflections of life, we find our true place.

## Fragments of a Sunlit Tomorrow

In droplets of morning, the sun starts to weave,
The fabric of dreams that the night had conceived.
With golden-tongued whispers, it lights up the morn,
In fragments of sunlit, new hopes are reborn.

Each ray a reminder, that shadows can't stay,
As colors unfold in a bright, beautiful way.
The world stirs awake, in the warm embrace near,
In fragments of sunlight, we banish our fear.

Clouds drift like dreams, in a quilt of soft hues,
As laughter breaks free from the morning's sweet muse.
With every heart swelling, like sails on the sea,
In fragments of sunlit, we learn to feel free.

So gather these moments, let them fill your soul,
For in the sun's glow, we find we are whole.
In each glimmering piece, we craft our own lane,
In fragments of sunlight, we dance through the rain.

With joy as our beacon, we journey ahead,
Embracing each moment, our fears left for dead.
Together we'll savor, the promise, the glow,
In fragments of sunlit tomorrow, we'll grow.

## Glimmers of Eternity on the Breeze

In whispers soft, the shadows dance,
Bright glimmers spark with a fleeting chance.
The world awakes in twilight's glow,
As hope ignites, and dreams bestow.

Across the field, the blossoms sway,
With laughter sweet, they greet the day.
A breeze hums tunes lost in time,
Nature's heart, in harmony, chime.

Beneath the stars, we weave our dreams,
In silver threads, entwined it seems.
Each breath, a step toward the divine,
In every heartbeat, a fragile sign.

But shadows linger, soft as night,
We chase the echoes, fading light.
In every corner, memories arise,
Like shimmering secrets in starlit skies.

A journey forged in whispered sighs,
Where hopes entwine, and love never dies.
For in this realm, where magic lies,
The heart ignites, and the spirit flies.

# Unraveling the Threads of Twilight

In twilight's grasp, we weave the tale,
Of dreams embraced, where shadows sail.
The horizon blushes, a tender hue,
As day surrenders, sweet and true.

Gentle winds carry secrets old,
Through echoing realms, their stories told.
With every whisper, a thread unwinds,
Linking the hearts of curious minds.

Beneath the gaze of the watchful moon,
Time sways gently, a lilting tune.
We gather starlight in our hands,
In this moment, forever stands.

The tapestry of dusk is spun,
With colors bright, as day is done.
Each fleeting second, a precious thread,
In the loom of life, where dreams are bred.

As night descends, we find our way,
Through labyrinths of the skies' ballet.
The strands entwined, we boldly tread,
In twilight's embrace, where fears are shed.

# Shattered Reflections in Midnight Waters

In the stillness of the moonlit lake,
Shattered whispers, the waters awake.
Glimmers of truth, in ripples they lie,
Beneath the surface, secrets sigh.

With every wave, a story breaks,
A haunting melody that fate awakes.
Stars like diamonds, scattered and bright,
Dance in the depths of the endless night.

The echoes linger, a ghostly refrain,
Of laughter lost, and lingering pain.
Reflections ripple, then fade from view,
A tapestry woven with shades of blue.

In midnight's glow, we seek the past,
Each shimmering image, a spell it casts.
The heart remembers what the mind forgets,
In the quietude, a world begets.

So dive within, and seek the spark,
Where shadows dance in the still and dark.
For in the depths, we find our way,
In shattered reflections, our spirits sway.

# The Celestial Choir's Soft Refrain

On starlit paths, where shadows play,
The celestial choir sings a ballet.
Notes like whispers, they drift and swell,
In harmony woven, a timeless spell.

With each soft chord, the heavens sigh,
Their music rising, a lullaby.
In twilight's warmth, the soul takes flight,
On wings of dreams, through the velvet night.

Guided by stars, we dance in tune,
Beneath the glow of a watchful moon.
The universe cradles our secret desires,
In ethereal notes that spark our fires.

A symphony played on the strings of fate,
Each echo a promise, never too late.
In the silence between, where magic twirls,
The choir sings deep in the heart of worlds.

As dawn awakes, the notes will fade,
Yet in our hearts, the melody stayed.
For though the song may softly wane,
The spirit soars to the soft refrain.

## Flames of Resilience in Soft Color

In twilight's embrace, hope softly glows,
With whispers of strength where the wild river flows.
The embers of dreams, they flicker and sway,
Lighting the shadows that darken the day.

Courage, a dance on the edge of the night,
Wrapped in the warmth of a promise held tight.
Each flicker, a story, each spark, a new song,
In the heart of the brave, where all souls belong.

Through colors of sorrow and shades of delight,
Resilience blooms in the dawn's early light.
A canvas of passion, where shy heartbeats meet,
Together they rise, unyielding and sweet.

Like petals that gather the dawn's gentle dew,
They whisper of battles, both fragile and true.
In the flames of their spirit, they forge what they crave,
A tapestry woven, from love, bold and brave.

So sing, oh sweet fire, in hues soft yet bright,
For in every flicker, there lies human might.
A harmony crafted from laughter and tears,
Together we stand, immune to our fears.

## The Laughter of Forgotten Stars

In a sky dusted silver with dreams long gone by,
Whispers of laughter weave low in the sigh.
Forgotten yet gleaming, they twinkle and tease,
A symphony echoed on the soft evening breeze.

Each flickering glow tells a tale of its own,
Of warmth and of wonder, of hearts that have grown.
In shadows once lost, now a glimmer's embrace,
A reminder that joy is a dance we all trace.

With stardust as laughter, they shimmer and sway,
Creating new pathways in the bright Milky Way.
In the quiet of night, their warmth we revive,
As dreams intertwine, together we thrive.

For time may conceal but can never erase,
The magic that flows in the vastness of space.
So laugh with the stars, let your spirit rejoice,
In the echo of laughter, hear the universe's voice.

A tapestry woven from sorrow and cheer,
The stories of starlight we hold ever dear.
In the glow of forgotten, we find a new start,
Their laughter, our treasure - the joy of the heart.

# Serenity in the Color of Change

Amidst the soft hush of autumn's warm shade,
A whisper of calm in the moments we've made.
Leaves whisper secrets in colors untold,
As nature surrenders to silver and gold.

In cycles of time, we release and embrace,
The rhythm of life in a gentle, slow pace.
Each breeze sings of freedom, a soft, velvet grace,
As the world shifts and ripples, like fabric in space.

From chaos to stillness, we find our way home,
In the dance of the seasons, we're never alone.
For change is a canvas, both vibrant and vast,
We paint with our memories, both shadow and past.

Through twilight to dawn, let your heart understand,
That peace lies within like soft grains of sand.
In the colors of change, we foster our dreams,
And cherish each moment where life brightly gleams.

So breathe in the beauty, let stillness take hold,
For in every transition, a story unfolds.
Serenity whispers in shades bold and bright,
In the color of change, find your own guiding light.

# Rebirth Through Violet Veils

In gardens where shadows and light intertwine,
A soft purple glow spills, sweet and divine.
Cascading like whispers through petals of grace,
Violet veils beckon, inviting embrace.

A hush in the stillness, where silence can sing,
Each heartbeat a promise, a future in spring.
From ashes we rise, where the past gently fades,
In the warmth of new blossoms, the soul serenades.

Through shadows once heavy, new colors unfold,
The stories of growth in the whispers retold.
In the depths of the night, where we seek and we dream,
Rebirth through the veils; how wondrous it seems!

So dance with the twilight, and twirl in the breeze,
For life is a journey, a flow, and it frees.
Embrace every moment, each dawn shining bright,
In violet's soft glow, find your spirit's true light.

With hope as your compass, the heart learns to soar,
Through cycles of time, to what's waiting in store.
Rebirth is a treasure, a promise we weave,
In the folds of the violet, our hearts learn to believe.

## In the Glow of Sacred Cinders

Amidst the piles of whispering ash,
The secrets speak in amber flash.
Each flicker warms a lost despair,
In glowing embers, hope lays bare.

Underneath the starry sweep,
The echoes of the past still weep.
In every crackle, tales arise,
Of dreams ignited in midnight skies.

Glimmers dance on ancient stone,
A hearth where shadows find a home.
The fire's heart remembers all,
As night descends and shadows fall.

With every spark, a wish takes flight,
Sending whispers into the night.
Hold tight the moments, let them fly,
In sacred glow, your spirit sighs.

So gather 'round the crackling blaze,
Awash in warmth, in fiery haze.
For in this light, the truth is found,
In sacred cinders, hope is crowned.

## Timeless Echoes Beyond the Veil

Through misty paths where shadows roam,
Lie whispers soft, of lost at home.
Timeless echoes, sweet refrain,
In silent songs, they call our names.

With every step the world may fade,
And memories twist in twilight's shade.
Yet in the stillness, breathe the air,
In every moment, spirits care.

From stars that twinkle, dreams descend,
In cosmic threads, our journeys blend.
Beyond the veil where silence sighs,
The heart can see with wiser eyes.

So linger long in twilight's grace,
Find solace in this sacred space.
For every echo, bright and clear,
Reminds us of those we hold dear.

In timeless chords, we weave our muse,
An endless dance, where fate won't lose.
Through every heartbeat, every breath,
We find the life beyond the death.

# Elysian Shades in Urban Gardens

In concrete jungles where shadows lie,
Elysian shades drift softly by.
With tender blooms in hidden nooks,
Nature whispers through old books.

Each petal holds a world serene,
In vibrant hues, a tranquil scene.
Amongst the bustle, hearts can sway,
In urban gardens, peace will stay.

Underneath the arching trees,
The laughter dances on the breeze.
A sanctuary, soft and bright,
In every corner, pure delight.

So find the beauty in the gray,
Where flowers bloom and children play.
In Elysium's embrace, we find,
The city's pulse so sweet, so kind.

For even here, in life's parade,
The heart of nature won't soon fade.
With open arms, it gently sways,
In urban gardens, time obeys.

## Mosaic of Dreams Beneath the Stars

Beneath the sky, a canvas vast,
A mosaic of dreams, shadows cast.
With every twinkle, wishes light,
Embroidered tales in the cloak of night.

Each star a chance, each blink a hope,
A universe where hearts can cope.
In this vastness, we lay our claims,
On the shimmering quilt of names.

The whispers of the cosmos call,
With secrets sown in the twilight's thrall.
In every hush, a heartbeat grows,
In cosmic winds, the spirit flows.

So reach up high and take a flight,
On dreams that shimmer, pure and bright.
With open eyes and a yearning heart,
We find our place, we play our part.

For in the night, as dreams unfold,
A tapestry of tales retold.
Mosaic moments, forever spun,
Beneath the stars, we are all one.

# Embers of Dreams in the Quiet

In the stillness of midnight's grasp,
Whispers of wishes softly weave.
Stars flicker like embers in the dark,
Cradling secrets that hearts believe.

Through shadows where silence resides,
The night cradles tales untold.
Beneath the gaze of an ancient moon,
Dreams gather, shimmering like gold.

Lost in the echoes of slumbering thoughts,
Hope dances on the edge of despair.
Each ember a memory, glowing bright,
A promise that lingers in the air.

Embers that flicker, then softly fade,
Yet in their warmth, we find our way.
Awakening moments, tugging at hearts,
In the quiet, they long to stay.

The dawn approaches, casting a light,
And with it, the dreams slowly wane.
Yet held in the depths of the twilight's fold,
Embers will spark once again.

## Navigating the Celestial Seas

On ships of the starlit ocean bright,
We sail through the velvet night sky.
Stars are our beacons, guiding our path,
As constellations whisper and sigh.

With sails of silver and dreams to unfold,
We chase after galaxies far.
The cosmos hums in a rhythm divine,
And each twinkle's a gift from a star.

Waves of stardust crash against our bows,
While comets blaze trails of fire.
We dance with the planets, spin with the moons,
In a ballet that stirs the desire.

Navigating realms both strange and profound,
We revel in wonders untamed.
In the tapestry of night's endless stretch,
Each moment forever named.

And though we may drift on celestial tides,
Our hearts anchor deep in the dream.
For in every ripple, in every star,
A universe whispers, it seems.

## Echoes of Laughter at Dusk's End

As daylight draws its final breath,
Laughter lingers on the breeze.
Children's giggles, a soft embrace,
Paint dusk in shades of memories.

In the glow of the sinking sun,
Echoes ripple through the trees.
Whispers of joy, a symphony sweet,
Entwined with the rustling leaves.

Long shadows stretch across the ground,
As twilight swirls in hues of gold.
The world grows softer in twilight's grasp,
While secrets of laughter slowly unfold.

A dance of fireflies in gentle dusk,
Their flickers mirror the joy inside.
With every breeze, a chuckle flows,
In the fading warmth, our hearts abide.

And as the stars begin to wake,
We carry laughter in our souls.
For even as night claims the day,
The echoes of joy forever extol.

## Venusian Dances in a Smoky Sky


In the depths of a smoky twilight,
Whirls of color begin to unfold.
Venus spins in its radiant ball,
A dance in the heavens, vibrant and bold.

Glimmers of pink and violet hues,
Weave tales of longing in the air.
Each twirl is a whisper, a secret kept,
With fragrant stars lingering there.

Clouds embrace in a tender sway,
As night steals the glow of the day.
Venusian spirits rise and fall,
In this celestial ballet, they play.

In smoky veils of the dreamy dusk,
They twirl through the warmth of the night.
Delight dances where shadows converge,
And hearts flutter in shared delight.

So let us join in this cosmic waltz,
With every step, a promise made.
In the smoky embrace of the evening star,
Together, we'll never fade.

# Resounding Radiance After the Storm

In the hush that follows the rain,
Whispers of light dance again.
Silver droplets kiss the ground,
Nature's harmony, a joyful sound.

Clouds retreat in soft retreat,
Sunbeams weave a path so sweet.
Buds awaken, fresh and bright,
A world reborn in golden light.

The sky blushes with hues of grace,
As time restores its tender pace.
Life rejoices, shadows cease,
In this moment, hearts find peace.

Echoes of laughter fill the air,
Dreams take flight, beyond despair.
From ashes rise a radiant hue,
A testament to all we've been through.

Embrace the dawn, let spirits rise,
Wonders unfolding beneath clear skies.
With every step in this sacred space,
We find our way, guided by grace.

# Twilight's Embrace on Phoenix Ashes

As twilight whispers soft goodbyes,
Stars awaken in velvet skies.
From ashes old, the fire takes flight,
A phoenix born from deepest night.

Colors blend in twilight's glow,
With every shadow, secrets flow.
The world turns soft in muted hues,
Where dreams emerge and hope renews.

Magic lingers in the breeze,
Awakening souls with gentle ease.
In the dance of dusk, we find our way,
To forge new paths at the close of day.

So let us gather, hand in hand,
In twilight's arms, a promised land.
With hearts ignited, we shall rise,
To claim the light beyond the skies.

Every ember carries a tale,
Of strength renewed when all seems frail.
Trust in the dawn, the cycle spins,
From ashes rise, let the journey begin.

# A Symphony of Rebirth and Light

In the symphony of morning's grace,
Every note finds its rightful place.
A chorus blooms with vibrant cheer,
As life awakens, drawing near.

With each heartbeat, a rhythm flows,
Nature's dance in soft repose.
Fingers of sunlight play through trees,
Whispering secrets carried by the breeze.

The world transforms in bursts of color,
Life unfurls, each moment a treasure.
From barren soil, green shoots appear,
With hope reborn, we cast off fear.

Listen close, the earth's refrain,
A melody rich, both joy and pain.
Together we rise, hand in hand,
Creating harmony across the land.

Let each heartbeat be a spark,
Guiding us through the dark.
In the symphony of life's embrace,
We find our truth in a sacred space.

## Nights Drenched in Sapphire Glow

Beneath the canopy of night's embrace,
Sapphire dreams take their rightful place.
The moon spills silver on velvet dreams,
Guiding us through soft, starlit streams.

With shadows cast, the world stands still,
Embracing silence, a gentle thrill.
Each twinkle echoes wishes made,
In the tapestry of night's parade.

The sky awakens enigmatic tales,
Of distant lands and whispered gales.
With every breath, a secret shared,
In sapphire glow, our souls laid bare.

As constellations weave through realms,
We seek the truth that love compels.
Together we wander through the night,
Bathed in magic, hearts alight.

So let us dance under cosmic glow,
In the embrace of the night we know.
For in these moments, pure and bright,
We find our dreams take daring flight.

# Silhouettes in the Horizon's Embrace

In twilight's grasp, where shadows play,
Figures lean, as night meets day.
Whispers dance on a breath of wind,
Secrets kept where dreams begin.

Stars awaken, one by one,
Each a tale that's just begun.
Echoes of laughter fill the air,
Silhouettes linger, unaware.

Clouds drift softly, painted gold,
Stories of old that once were told.
The horizon stretches, vast and wide,
Embracing all, a gentle guide.

Moments fleeting, lost in time,
Caught within a fading rhyme.
As darkness settles, hearts entwine,
Beneath the sky, a world divine.

## The Gentle Rise of Spectral Light

In softest hues, the dawn awakes,
A gentle rise, the silence breaks.
Colors blend, a painter's dream,
Sketching life in each soft beam.

Misty whispers float on high,
Brightly draped across the sky.
The world beneath begins to stir,
Nature's breath, a gentle purr.

Birds take flight on wings of fire,
Chasing light, their hearts aspire.
Every note, a song of grace,
Welcoming warmth in this vast space.

As shadows fade and hope ignites,
The canvas brightens, pure delights.
In gentle rise, our souls take flight,
Embracing all, the spectral light.

**Fragments of Dawn across the Canvas**

With every brush of morning's hand,
Fragments of dawn across the land.
Glimmers spark on dewy ground,
A masterpiece, in silence found.

Hues of crimson, amber, gold,
A story waiting to be told.
Each stroke speaks of hope anew,
A moment's breath, a vibrant hue.

The horizon yawns, a gentle sigh,
As daylight spills from the sky.
Nature's palette, rich and rare,
Awakens thoughts, floating in air.

Petals open, kissed by light,
Embracing warmth, dispelling night.
Across the canvas, life complies,
In fragments found, the heart complies.

# Fleeting Moments Wrapped in Color

Fleeting moments, time unwinds,
Wrapped in color, joy finds.
A child's laughter, a breeze so sweet,
Life's simple pleasures, pure and complete.

Painting dreams in shades of blue,
Memories cherished, bright and true.
Colors whisper of days gone by,
As sunlight kisses the morning sky.

Crimson sunsets, vibrant and bold,
Embrace the stories that we hold.
Every heartbeat, a pulse of grace,
In fleeting moments, love we trace.

With canvas wide, we find our song,
In fleeting color where we belong.
Life's transient dance, a sweet ballet,
Wrapped in moments that fade away.

# Beneath the Azure Horizon

In whispers light the azure we see,
Waves embrace the shore's gentle plea.
Clouds drift softly, like dreams on the rise,
Beneath the vastness of endless skies.

The sun dips low, painting gold on the sea,
A world awakened, wild and free.
Birds take flight, their songs fill the air,
A melody woven, for those who dare.

With every tide, a secret unfolds,
Stories of sailors and treasures untold.
Stars will shimmer as night takes its throne,
Guiding the wanderers, never alone.

Mountains stand tall, guardians of light,
Casting shadows that dance through the night.
In moments of stillness, wisdom will bloom,
A quiet reminder, there's beauty in gloom.

So here in this place, where skies ever gleam,
Hope is a lantern, a flickering dream.
Beneath the azure, where hearts intertwine,
We chase the horizon, and in it, we shine.

# Embers of a Celestial Bloom

A touch of twilight ignites the dark skies,
With embers sparking, where wonder lies.
Stars like whispers dance through the void,
In the garden of night, where dreams are deployed.

Each flicker of light tells a tale of old,
Of heroes and journeys, of spirits bold.
Moonlight drapes softly, a silvery shroud,
Embracing the heart of a sleeping crowd.

Petals of stardust begin to unfurl,
In the night's embrace, a magical swirl.
The cosmos awakens, fresh stories to weave,
In the tapestry of fate, we dare to believe.

Time drifts like shadows, a delicate breeze,
Carrying whispers through rustling leaves.
In the dance of the cosmos, all sorrows unmoor,
With embers of hope, we rise to explore.

Through the veil of the night, our spirits will soar,
Kindled by dreams, forever we'll adore.
For in each celestial bloom, lies a spark,
A reminder that love lights the way through the dark.

## Canvas of Serenity Unfolding

In the hush of dawn, where silence sings clear,
A canvas of calm begins to appear.
Brushstrokes of colors, soft shades intertwine,
Awakening whispers, in rhythms divine.

Morning dew glistens like jewels on the grass,
As sunlight peeks in, the shadows do pass.
Nature's embrace, so tender and sweet,
In moments of stillness, our hearts feel complete.

A breeze carries stories, of earth and of sky,
Painting the world as the day lingers by.
Each petal and leaf dances with grace,
In the symphony of life, we find our own place.

Cascading waters sing lullabies soft,
In pools of tranquility, souls can aloft.
With the rhythm of waves that gently caress,
Here in this haven, we find our success.

So let us unwind in this tranquil array,
Where peace writes the verses of each passing day.
For in the embrace of serenity's glow,
We discover the magic in letting love flow.

# The Dance of a Forgotten Sky

Once vibrant stars flickered, now dimmed by time,
In the dance of a sky, both tender and prime.
Echoes of laughter, carried by breeze,
Whisper through shadows, like ancient trees.

A tapestry woven in colors once bright,
Now fades into shades of an endless night.
Yet within the silence, a spark still remains,
A heartbeat of memory that still wanes.

Each twilight tells stories of love's bitter end,
Yet hope lingers softly, as time can amend.
For even in darkness, there's beauty unseen,
In the dance of forgotten, the places we've been.

When clouds drift apart, revealing the glow,
Old constellations begin to bestow.
The dreams we once harbored, ignited anew,
In the depths of the dusk, we venture through.

So let's hold these moments, though faded their hue,
In the dance of the sky, our spirits renew.
For every lost star sings of journeys untold,
In the embrace of the night, we find our home bold.

## The Melodies of Starlit Sojourns

In twilight whispers, secrets play,
The night unveils her silver sway.
Each star a note, in cosmic tune,
We dance beneath the watchful moon.

With shadows long and laughter bright,
We wander forth, in dream's delight.
A journey through the velvet sky,
Where wishes soar, and spirits fly.

The breeze, it brings a gentle sound,
As crickets sing, the night surrounds.
In every heart, a timeless cheer,
The magic stirs, so close, yet near.

A tapestry of dreams and light,
We catch the stars, they twinkle bright.
With every step, our souls entwine,
In starlit realms, our joys align.

So let us chase the dawn anew,
With melodies that spark the view.
For in the night, our spirits roam,
In starlit dreams, we find our home.

## Wonders Beyond Time's Grasp

In ancient tales where magic flows,
The whispers weave through time's exposed.
With every breath, the history sings,
Of dreams that touch our fleeting wings.

Through swirling mists of yesteryear,
We hold the stories, crystal clear.
The echoes dance in shadowed light,
As time reveals its wondrous flight.

Each moment sparks a brand new chance,
In every heart, a secret dance.
We glimpse the threads of fate's embrace,
In every heart, a timeless grace.

The past, a canvas painted bold,
With colors rich and stories told.
Through ages lost, our spirits soar,
To grasp the magic evermore.

So let us dream of worlds unseen,
Where time stands still, and hearts convene.
In every pause, a wonder wakes,
Beyond the grasp, our spirit takes.

# Kaleidoscope of Lost Wishes

In chambers deep where wishes sigh,
A kaleidoscope of dreams draw nigh.
The colors swirl, a vibrant hue,
As hope awakens, bold and true.

Each wish a petal, soft and bright,
Twirling gently in the night.
With every glance, a memory flares,
In whispered tones, the heart declares.

Through tangled paths of what might be,
We journey on, and spirit free.
The echoes of our dreams entwine,
Creating worlds, a grand design.

A mosaic of the lost and found,
In every fragment, love is crowned.
We piece together every gleam,
In a tapestry of hope, a dream.

So chase the glimmer of the night,
Embrace the shadows, hearts ignite.
For in this dance of wishes lost,
We find our way, no matter the cost.

# Rays of Hope in a Starry Veil

Beneath the stars, a gentle light,
A veil of hope that warms the night.
Each glimmer brings a promise near,
In shadows deep, we have no fear.

The heavens hum a soft refrain,
As dreams awaken from their chain.
A symphony of light and grace,
In every heart, we find our place.

With every star, a wish is spun,
A tale of hope just begun.
We stand together, side by side,
In unity, our spirits glide.

A radiant warmth against the chill,
With love and kindness, we fulfill.
In cosmic threads, our stories weave,
The night adorns what we believe.

So let us raise our gaze above,
In starlit skies, we find our love.
For every ray that shines so bright,
Holds whispers sweet of endless light.

www.ingramcontent.com/pod-product-compliance
Ingram Content Group UK Ltd.
Pitfield, Milton Keynes, MK11 3LW, UK
UKHW021445290125
4349UKWH00039B/633